Introduction

Start With Scraps is not just another scrap book. This book will actually help your scrap collection disappear. There will be little waste as you make your own fabric by piecing your scraps together. The scrappy-piecing technique explained here is fast and fun. Once you start scrappy piecing, you won't want to stop!

All the projects in the book are easy to sew and economical. You no doubt already have all the materials needed for the projects, which will help shrink your stash of scraps and make room for new fabrics!

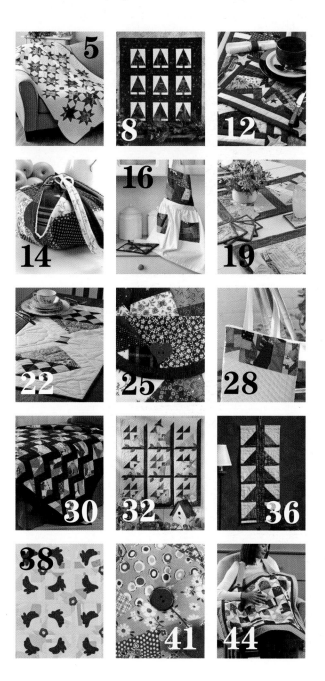

Table of Contents

2   Start With Scraps

2   Meet the Designer

3   Basic Instructions

5   Now Starring: Leftovers

8   Pieceful Pines

12   Crazy for the Red, White & Blue Set

14   Casserole Carrier

16   Kitchen Leftovers

19   Garden Snippets

22   Grandmother's Scrap Basket Table Runner

25   Tiny Totes

28   Scrappy Tote Bag

30   Striking!

32   Flocking Together

36   Association Meeting

38   Joy!

41   Little Leftovers

44   Scraps Squared Nursing Cover

Start With Scraps

Scraps, scraps, scraps! The more you quilt and sew, the more scraps you accumulate. Each completed project generates leftovers—fabric scraps that are just too big to throw away. Most likely these scraps get stuffed into bags or boxes with scraps from previous projects. These bags and boxes seem to multiply or end up bulging. Soon they are taking over your sewing room. In an attempt to clean out and organize, you are tempted to just give or throw them away—wait!

Think back to your grandmother and her mother before her. Their scrap bags were their main source of fabrics for quilts. Truly one-of-a-kind quilts were made from those scrap bags. Looking at those old quilts is like looking at a fabric collection of the time—or of several generations. And if you look carefully, you can see clever ways in which small pieces were sewn together to make one piece large enough to complete a design. Also noticeable is the fact that if Grandma did not have enough of one fabric to complete her quilt, she simply continued on with another fabric of a similar shade.

Unique quilts can be made from your scraps too. There are a lot of scrap-quilt patterns available. Most of these require you to cut your scraps into pieces of a specific size and shape. Doing this only generates more scraps!

Why not just use the scraps as they are? By piecing the scraps together, you can make your own fabric. Then, from this fabric, you can cut the size and shape pieces you need. The scraps that are generated from this technique will be small enough that you can throw them away without feeling guilty.

All of the projects in this book are started in this way. Take some time to look at them. Each one uses a slightly different assortment of scraps.

Please read through all instructions before beginning any project and refer to the Basic Instructions as needed.

Meet the Designer

Carol Loessel has had a passion for quilting for over 50 years. This passion began at an early age when she slept under quilts her grandma lovingly stitched. From then on, she had the desire to learn how to sew and eagerly acquired all the sewing knowledge she could from her mother and grandmothers. Since the 1970s Carol has been quilting and accumulating scraps. Her favorite quilts are traditional ones, the scrappier the better. Carol's idea for scrapping was born out of the fact that she simply cannot bear to part with even the smallest piece of fabric. She is a former elementary school teacher who enjoys inspiring others by sharing her knowledge of quilts and quilt-making through lectures and classes. In the past few years, Carol has published patterns for her original designs. Carol Loessel resides in Macomb, Mich., with her husband. She has two grown daughters and two young granddaughters who stay warm at night under quilts that she has designed and stitched with love. For more information, e-mail Carol at cloessel@yahoo.com or visit her blog at www.scrapquiltmakerdesigner.blogspot.com.

Basic Instructions

All of the projects in this book refer you to these instructions to make the scrappy patchwork. Get familiar with the process before you start a project.

Getting Started

To begin, you need to find out exactly what you have in your scrap collection. This probably means doing some cleaning in your sewing room. Pull out all the boxes and bags of scraps you have stashed away there. Also bring out any quilt-project left-overs you find.

Take your scrap bags and boxes to a place where you have room to work. Have a wastebasket handy. Dump out the bags and boxes, and start sorting.

First of all, look for pieces of fabric that will be large enough to work with. Remember that a ¼" seam allowance is needed all around a scrap of fabric. If not much fabric is left after the seam allowance is taken, discard the scrap. A lot of seams in a small area will create too much bulk for later seaming or quilting. (If you do appliqué work, smaller scraps might be useful for that.)

Sort out long strips and small squares to be used in other scrap-quilt projects. Triangles will work fine here. Already pieced-together chunks from previous quilt borders or blocks are fun additions too. The most interesting projects in this collection are ones made from odd-shaped or previously pieced scraps.

At this point, make several different piles:

   Strips—long ones, to be used in another project

   Squares—small ones, to be used in another project

   Small pieces—too small for these projects, but to be saved for appliqué

   Scraps of a good size— just right for these projects

   Shares—those not of interest to you, but that others might like

   Throw-aways—into the wastebasket right away

Put away the long strips (great for a string quilt). Put away the small squares (great for a Four-Patch quilt). Put away the small pieces you are saving for appliqué. Perhaps organize a "Swap-n-Share" with other quilting friends to trade scraps.

Now take a good look at your pile of good-size scraps. What colors do you notice most? Think about which project you'd like to make. What colors will you need?

If you are just mixing colors and fabrics, perhaps no further sorting is necessary.

If you want to stick to one color palette, start sorting by colors. Put all the neutrals (white, gray, beige, pastels) in one pile. Make a pile for all of the greens. Make another pile for all of the blues. Make another pile for all of the reds, and so on.

Thinking about a certain theme for your quilt? If you want a Christmas quilt, sort out all the reds, greens and creams/whites. If you want a fall quilt, sort out the yellows, browns, greens, oranges, rusts, etc. A baby quilt might use light versions of pinks, blues, greens, yellows and purples.

Once the scraps are sorted, re-package and label them. Place them in clear zipper bags or clear plastic totes so you can see what you have. Save out the scraps you have chosen to work with for your project.

The Scrappy-Piecing Technique

The scraps are prepared and pieced in the same way for each of the projects in this collection.

Take your chosen scraps to the ironing board and press them thoroughly. After pressing, they will stay flat if you put them into a large, flat box.

Tips

A ¼" seam allowance is used for all projects unless otherwise noted.

Press seam allowances open when joining squares of scrappy-pieced fabric.

Scrappy-pieced fabric is busy. Use a solid or a fabric that reads like a solid in the sashings or other surrounding pieces. Let the scrappy-pieced fabric be the focal point of the quilt or project.

In order to have a flat piece of fabric to work with once all the scraps are sewn together, it is necessary to have a straight edge to follow when sewing. Using your rotary cutter and long ruler, trim one straight edge on each scrap. It does not matter which edge you straighten, and pay no attention to the grain of the fabric. Choose to straighten the edge where you will be removing the LEAST amount of fabric. Throw away the cut-off pieces.

The scraps are pieced together randomly, combining them by the length of the cut edge. Lay two scraps right sides together with the straight edge of the top scrap on the right. Place the top scrap right sides together on the bottom one in such a way that the length of the cut side matches the length of a section of the bottom scrap (this does not necessarily have to be its cut edge).

(See Photo 1) Match up several sets of scraps in this way before sewing any. Stack them alongside your sewing machine. When you are ready to sew, chain-piece the sets, feeding them one right after the other under your presser foot.

Photo 1

Sew the seam following the cut edge of the top scrap with the edge of your machine's presser foot, using (approximately) a ¼" seam allowance. Trim the bottom scrap even with the cut edge of the top scrap.

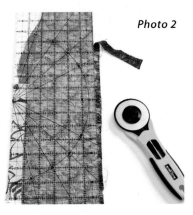

Photo 2

(See Photo 2) If the cut-off part is large enough, save it to piece to another scrap. If it is not large enough, discard it. Press the seam allowance to one side.

Trim a straight edge on the newly pieced sets. Match these cut edges to those of other sets or other scraps and piece together again. Continue putting together scraps in this way until you have a large piece of fabric.

Check the pattern you are using to see what size unit you need to cut from your scrappy-pieced fabric. Piece enough fabric to cut three or four of these units. You will have leftover cut-off pieces. Do not discard these. Work these into the next set of scraps you are piecing together.

Piece enough fabric to be able to cut out the number of units specified in the pattern.

Put the leftovers away for your next project.

Continue with your chosen pattern as directed.

A Few Helpful Hints

- When working with large scraps of fabric, once a few of them are pieced together, cut the whole chunk into two or more pieces (the more angular the cut, the better). Mix these up by adding other scraps to each of them. This helps scatter the fabrics throughout the resulting squares to unify your quilt top. (See Photo 3)

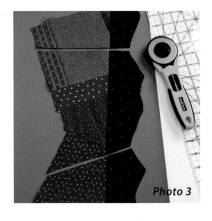

Photo 3

- Don't obsess over color placement. Use random color and fabric selection to make your quilt more interesting. Pulling your scraps out of a brown grocery sack without peeking is a good way to really mix things up.
- Using short strips? Add them at an angle for more interest. Or, piece several of them together, then cut a unique shape from them to piece into the rest.
- Use a small stitch length when doing the scrappy piecing.
- Use a neutral-color thread when doing the scrappy piecing—dark beige, gray, etc.
- If you find some especially thick seam allowances on the back of your scrappy-pieced fabric, check to see if you can carefully trim away some of the seam allowances.
- Handle cut pieces of scrappy-pieced fabric carefully. There are many different grains of fabric along the edges and you have to cut through lines of stitching.
- You are now ready to use your scrappy-pieced fabric in a project!

Now Starring: Leftovers

Scraps and quilt-top leftovers truly do shine as the centers of the Variable Star blocks. Chop them up, and then mix them up!

Project Specifications
Skill Level: Intermediate
Quilt Size: 51" x 76½"
Block Size: 8" x 8"
Number of Blocks: 38

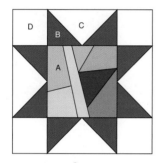

Star
8" x 8" Block
Make 38

Materials
- Variety of scraps for scrappy piecing
- 2⅛ yards blue mottled
- 3⅔ yards white tonal
- Batting 57" x 83"
- Backing 57" x 83"
- Neutral-color all-purpose thread
- Quilting thread
- Waster-soluble fabric marker
- Basic sewing tools and supplies

Cutting
1. Cut (10) 4½" by fabric width strips white tonal; subcut strips into (152) 2½" C rectangles.

2. Cut (10) 2½" by fabric width strips white tonal; subcut strips into (152) 2½" D squares.

3. Cut two 16½" by fabric width strips white tonal; subcut strips into (24) 2½" E strips.

4. Cut one 12⅝" by fabric width strip white tonal; subcut strip into three 12⅝" squares. Cut each square on both diagonals to make 12 G triangles.

5. Cut one 12¼" by fabric width strip white tonal; subcut strip into two 12¼" squares. Cut each square in half on one diagonal to make four H triangles.

6. Cut (20) 2½" by fabric width strips blue mottled; subcut strips into (311) B squares.

7. Cut one 4⅛" by fabric width strip blue mottled; subcut strip into three 4⅛" squares. Cut each square on both diagonals to make 12 F triangles; discard two.

8. Cut seven 2¼" by fabric width strips blue mottled for binding.

Making Scrappy-Pieced Sections
1. Using your chosen scraps and referring to the scrappy-piecing technique on page 3, make enough scrappy-pieced fabric to cut (38) 4½" x 4½" A squares.

Completing the Blocks
1. Draw a diagonal line from corner to corner on the wrong side of 304 B squares.

2. Layer a B square right sides together with C and stitch on the marked line as shown in Figure 1; trim seam allowance to ¼" and press B to the right side, again referring to Figure 1.

Figure 1

3. Repeat step 2 with B on the remaining end of C to complete one B-C unit as shown in Figure 2.

Figure 2

Figure 3

4. Repeat steps 2 and 3 to complete 152 B-C units.

5. To complete one Star block, sew a B-C unit to opposite sides of A to make the center row as shown in Figure 3; press seams toward A.

6. Sew a D square to opposite ends of a B-C unit as shown in Figure 4 to complete a row; press seams toward D. Repeat to make two rows.

Figure 4

7. Sew a row to the top and bottom of the center row to complete one Star block referring to the block drawing; press seams away from the center unit.

8. Repeat steps 5–7 to complete 38 Star blocks.

Completing the Top

1. Join two Star blocks to make a row; press seam in one direction. Repeat to make two rows; join the rows to make a four-block unit as shown in Figure 5; press seams in one direction. Repeat to make eight four-block units.

Figure 5

2. Join three four-block units with four E strips to make a row; press seams toward E strips. Repeat to make two three-unit rows.

3. Sew a G triangle to two adjacent sides of one Star block as shown in Figure 6 to make a side star unit; press seams toward G. Repeat to make six side star units.

Figure 6

4. Arrange and join the side star units with the four-block units, three-unit rows and the B, E and F pieces referring to Figure 7 for positioning; press seams toward sashing rows. Sew H triangles to each corner; press seams toward H to complete the pieced top.

Figure 7

Completing the Quilt

1. Sandwich the batting between the completed top and prepared backing; pin or baste layers together to hold.

2. Quilt as desired by hand or machine; remove pins or basting. Trim excess backing and batting even with quilt top.

3. Join binding strips on short ends with diagonal seams to make one long strip; trim seams to ¼" and press seams open. Fold the strip in half along length with wrong sides together; press.

4. Sew binding to the right side of the quilt edges, overlapping ends. Fold binding to the back side and stitch in place to finish. ❖

Now Starring: Leftovers
Placement Diagram 51" x 76½"

Tips

I use a lot of muslin in my projects. I like it and buy it by the bolt, so I have a lot of it on hand. If it is not your favorite, please feel free to substitute fabric that you do like.

When making templates, be sure to transfer all markings and information to the templates you make.

For small wall quilts, place mats and table runners, my favorite batting is Pellon fleece. It is flat and easy to quilt through by hand or machine.

Pieceful Pines

Gather up your greens to make the scrappy-pieced pine trees in this lap-size quilt.

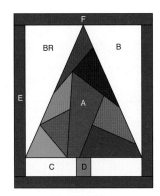

Pieceful Pine
9½" x 11½" Block
Make 9

Project Specifications
Skill Level: Intermediate
Quilt Size: 42½" x 48½"
Block Size: 9½" x 11½"
Number of Blocks: 9

Materials
- Assorted green scraps
- 1 fat quarter brown tonal
- ¾ yard dark green solid
- ⅞ yard cream tonal
- 1⅜ yards burgundy print
- Batting 49" x 55"
- Backing 49" x 55"
- All-purpose thread to match fabrics
- Water-soluble fabric marker
- Small-holed punch
- 9 (¾") gold star buttons
- Basic sewing tools and supplies

Making Scrappy-Pieced Sections
1. Using the assorted green scraps, follow the instructions for the scrappy-piecing technique found on page 3. Make enough scrappy-pieced fabric to cut nine A pieces referring to the following steps.

2. Prepare templates for A and B using patterns given; transfer all marks to the templates, and using a small-holed paper punch, punch holes at the dots on the template.

3. Place A on the right side of the scrappy-pieced fabric; place your ruler on the top of A, aligning the edge of the ruler with the edge of the template; cut out tree shapes.

4. Mark the dots through the punched holes on the wrong side of A pieces using a water-soluble fabric marker.

Cutting
1. Cut two 9¼" by fabric width strips cream tonal. Place the B template on the strip and cut nine each B and BR pieces as shown in Figure 1. Transfer the dots to the B and BR pieces using a water-soluble fabric marker.

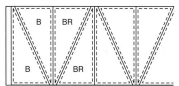

Figure 1

2. Cut one 4" by fabric width strip cream tonal; subcut strip into two 21" C strips.

3. Cut one 1½" x 21" D strip brown tonal.

4. Cut one 10½" by fabric width strip green solid; subcut strip into (18) 1¼" E strips.

5. Cut one 10" by fabric width strip green solid; subcut strip into (18) 1¼" F strips.

6. Cut four 3" by fabric width strips burgundy print; subcut strips into six 12" G sashing strips and two 34" H sashing strips.

7. Cut four 5" by fabric width I/J strips burgundy print.

8. Cut five 2¼" by fabric width strips burgundy print for binding.

Completing the Blocks
1. Sew the D strip between two C strips with right sides together along length; press seams toward D.

2. Subcut the C-D strip into nine 1¾" C-D units as shown in Figure 2.

Figure 2

3. To complete one Tree block, center and sew the C-D unit to the bottom or shortest edge of A; press seam toward A.

4. Sew B and BR to A, matching punched holes at corners; press seams toward B and BR.

5. Sew an E strip to opposite long sides and F strips to the top and bottom of the stitched unit; press seams toward E and F to complete one Tree block.

6. Repeat steps 3–6 to complete nine Tree blocks.

Completing the Top

1. Join three Tree blocks with two G strips to make a row; press seams toward G strips. Repeat to make three rows.

2. Join the rows with two H strips to complete the pieced center; press seams toward H strips.

3. Join the I/J strips on short ends to make one long strip; press seams open. Subcut strip into two 40" I strips and two 43" J strips.

4. Sew I strips to opposite long sides and J strips to the top and bottom of the pieced center; press seams toward I and J strips to complete the top.

Completing the Quilt

1. Sandwich the batting between the completed top and prepared backing; pin or baste layers together to hold.

2. Quilt as desired by hand or machine; remove pins or basting. Trim excess backing and batting even with quilt top.

3. Join binding strips on short ends with diagonal seams to make one long strip; trim seams to ¼" and press seams open. Fold the strip in half along length with wrong sides together; press.

4. Sew binding to the right side of the quilt edges, overlapping ends. Fold binding to the back side and stitch in place.

5. Sew a gold star button to the top of each tree to finish. ❖

B
Cut 18 cream tonal
(reverse half for BR)

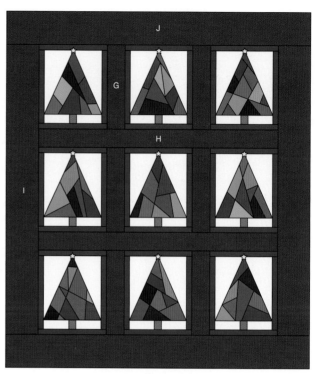

Pieceful Pines
Placement Diagram 42½" x 48½"

Chocolate Candy

This chocolate treat is quick to make. Replace some of the graham cracker crumbs with cereal crumbs for extra tastiness.

Ingredients
- 6 ounces chocolate mint chips, melted (½ of a 12-ounce package)
- ½ cup graham cracker crumbs
- 1 cup broken nuts

Mix all ingredients together. Drop by spoonfuls onto wax paper to cool and harden.

Other options: *Use regular chocolate chips, graham cracker crumbs, ¼ cup raisins and ¾ cup broken nut meats.*

Use milk chocolate chips. Substitute 1¼ cups shredded coconut for the nuts.

Barb's Free Beef Barley Soup
 Keep a container in the freezer; add leftover pot roast, gravy, vegetables, etc., to the
container. When the container is full, make soup:
 Brown ½ pound ground beef with ½ cup
onion. Drain. Add 4 cups water, ½ cup celery,
½ cup carrots, ¾ cup barley, 2 beef bouillon
cubes, 1 cup tomato juice, ½ tsp. basil and 1
bay leaf. Simmer until vegetables are tender.
Then add freezer container and extra frozen
vegetables as desired. Simmer until hot. Enjoy!

A
Cut 9 scrappy-pieced fabric

Crazy for the Red, White & Blue Set

Use these table accessories for your summer entertaining!

Project Specifications
Skill Level: Beginner
Runner Size: 42" x 15"
Place Mat Size: 18" x 12"

Materials to Make Runner and 2 Place Mats
- Assorted red, white and blue scraps
- 1 fat eighth navy solid
- 1 fat eighth gold solid
- ⅓ yard white solid
- ⅝ yard red solid
- 2 batting pieces 20" x 14"
- Batting 43" x 16"
- 2 backing pieces 20" x 14"
- Backing 43" x 16"
- All-purpose thread to match fabrics
- Basic sewing tools and supplies

Cutting
1. Cut (10) 1½" by fabric width C strips red solid.

2. Cut five 1½" by fabric width D strips white solid.

3. Cut (12) 3½" x 3½" E squares navy solid.

4. Prepare template for star; cut as directed, adding a ⅛"–¼" seam allowance for hand appliqué.

Making Scrappy-Pieced Sections
1. Using the assorted scraps, follow the instructions for the scrappy-piecing technique found on page 3. Make enough scrappy-pieced fabric to cut four 9½" x 9½" A squares and four 6½" x 6½" B squares.

Runner
1. Join the four A squares to make the pieced center; press seams open.

2. Sew a C strip to opposite sides of a D strip to make a C-D strip set; press seams toward C. Repeat to make five C-D strip sets.

3. Referring to Figure 1, subcut the C-D strip sets into two 9½" runner end strips and two 36½" runner side strips. Cut four 12½" place mat side strips and four 6½" place mat end strips; set aside place mat strips.

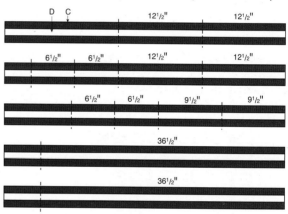

Figure 1

4. Sew a runner side strip to opposite long sides of the pieced center; press seams toward strips.

5. Center and hand-appliqué a star to each E square. Set aside eight squares for place mats.

6. Sew an appliquéd E square to each end of each runner end strip; press seams toward the E squares.

7. Sew an E/runner end strip to opposite short ends of the pieced center to complete the top.

8. Place the runner-size batting piece on a flat surface; place the stitched top right side up on the batting. Place the backing piece right sides together with the stitched top; pin and stitch layers together all around edges leaving a 4" opening on one side.

Crazy for the Red, White & Blue Runner
Placement Diagram 42" x 15"

9. Clip corners; trim backing and batting even with the edges of the runner top.

10. Turn runner right side out through opening, poking corners flat. Turn opening edges to the inside; hand-stitch opening closed. Press edges flat.

11. Quilt as desired to finish.

Place Mats

1. Join two B squares; press seam open. Repeat to make a second B unit.

2. Sew a place mat side strip to the long sides of the B units; press seams toward strips.

3. Repeat steps 6–11 for Completing the Runner to complete two place mats using place mat end strips, batting and backing. ❖

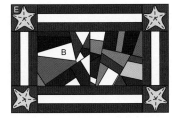

Crazy for the Red, White & Blue Place Mat
Placement Diagram 18" x 12"

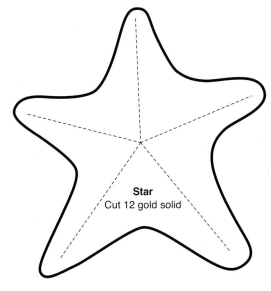

Star
Cut 12 gold solid

Casserole Carrier

Easy to make and fun to use, these carriers make great gifts.

Project Note
An insulated batting called Insul-Bright(R) is used inside to keep foods at just the right temperature.

Project Specifications
Skill Level: Beginner
Project Size: 17½" x 17½"

Materials
- Assorted scraps in desired colors
- 1⅝" x 24" scrap strip
- ⅝ yard muslin
- 18" x 18" square batting
- 2 strips batting 1⅝" x 24"
- Neutral-color all-purpose thread
- 2 (1½") bone rings
- 6½" round plate or lid
- Water-soluble fabric marker
- 2 (2½") pieces double-fold bias tape to match scrap colors
- Basic sewing tools and supplies

Cutting
1. Cut one 18" x 18" square muslin for lining.

2. Cut one 1⅝" x 24" strip muslin for handle lining.

Making Scrappy-Pieced Sections
1. Using the assorted scraps, follow the instructions for the scrappy-piecing technique found on page 3. Make enough scrappy-pieced fabric to cut four 9¼" x 9¼" A squares.

Completing the Casserole Cover
1. Join the four A squares to make a Four-Patch top referring to the Placement Diagram; press seams open.

2. Place the square of insulated batting on a flat surface; place the square of cotton batting on top. Place the muslin lining square right side up and the scrappy-pieced Four-Patch unit on top with wrong side up; pin the layers together.

3. Sew all around edges using a ¼" seam allowance, leaving a 4" opening on one side.

4. Trim corners; turn right side out through opening. Smooth out and press edges flat.

5. Turn in opening edge; hand-stitch opening closed.

6. Topstitch ⅝" from edge all around.

7. Center and trace around a 6½" small plate or plastic lid on the muslin side of the stitched carrier using a water-soluble fabric marker. Stitch along the traced line; remove markings.

Making Handles
1. Place the two 1⅝" x 24" batting strips on a flat surface; place the same-size muslin strip on the batting strips right side up. Place the fabric handle strip on top with wrong side up; pin the layers together.

2. Sew all around edges using a ¼" seam allowance, leaving a 4" opening along one side for turning.

3. Trim corners; turn right side out. Smooth edges; press. Turn opening edges to the inside; hand-stitch opening closed.

4. Topstitch down the center and ⅜" from each side of the handle.

5. Attach handle to opposite diagonal corners on the patchwork side of the carrier referring to Figure 1; secure stitching with a second row of stitching on top of the first.

Figure 1

6. Slip one end of one piece of the double-fold bias tape through one bone ring; fold bias tape in half with raw ends together forming a loop to hold the ring as shown in Figure 2.

Figure 2

7. Sew the ends of the bias tape to the scrappy side of the carrier ⅝" from edge and 1" from corner on

one of the remaining corners as shown in Figure 3; secure stitching with a second row of stitching on top of the first.

Figure 3

8. Repeat steps 6 and 7 with the remaining bias tape and bone ring on the remaining corner.

9. Pull the rings toward the corners, bringing bias loop over the raw bias ends. Move ring down and out of the way as shown in Figure 4. Stitch close to the fold of the bias near the carrier corner; stitch again over first stitching.

Figure 4

Using the Casserole Carrier
1. Set a casserole in the center of the carrier square; fold the handle in half at the center and slip the rings, one at a time, over the folded handle. Carry with the handle. ❖

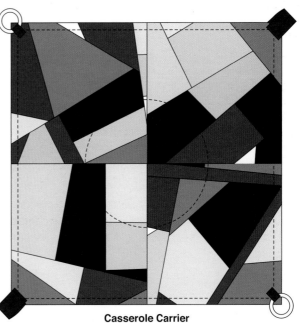

Casserole Carrier
Placement Diagram 17½" x 17½"

Kitchen Leftovers

This simple apron and pot holder are great for gift-giving.

Project Specifications
Skill Level: Beginner
Apron Size: 1 size fits all
Pot Holder Size: 8½" x 8½"

Materials
- Assorted scraps in chosen colors
- 1 yard good-quality muslin
- 8½" x 8½" square backing fabric
- 8½" x 8½" square cotton batting
- 8½" x 8½" square insulated batting
- All-purpose thread to match fabrics
- 1 package extra-wide double-fold bias tape to contrast with scraps
- Basic sewing tools and supplies

Cutting
1. Cut one 18½" x 38" muslin for skirt piece.

2. Cut one 10½" x 10½" apron bib square and two 6" x 6" pocket lining squares muslin.

3. Cut the following from the remaining muslin: two 3" x 24" ties, two 2½" x 24" waistbands and two 2½" x 23" neck ties.

Making Scrappy-Pieced Sections
1. Using the assorted scraps, follow the instructions for the scrappy-piecing technique found on page 3. Make enough scrappy-pieced fabric to cut one 10½" x 10½" A square and two 6" x 6" B squares.

Apron

Note: All seams are ¼" unless otherwise directed.

1. Fold one 2½" x 23" neck tie strip in half with right sides together along length; stitch along one end and the long side.

2. Turn strip right side out; press. Topstitch ⅛" away from all edges.

3. Repeat steps 1 and 2 for other neck tie.

4. Select the top edge of the bib A square; pin neck ties to the top edge of A ¼" in from the side edges with raw edges even as shown in Figure 1.

Figure 1

5. Pin the 10½" x 10½" bib lining piece right sides together with the bib A square. Sew layers together along two sides and the top edge. *Note: Be careful not to catch the side edges of the neck ties in your stitching.*

6. Trim corners; turn bib right side out, poke out corners and smooth edges. Press edges flat; topstitch along the three stitched sides.

7. Mark the center of the bottom edge of the bib.

8. Press under ¼" on each short edge of the skirt piece; turn under ¼" again and press. Stitch close to the fold on each edge.

9. Along one long edge (bottom of skirt), press under 1", then 1" again; stitch close to folded edge.

10. Mark the center top edge of the skirt piece.

11. Pin one scrappy-pieced B square right sides together with a 6" pocket-lining square; stitch all around, leaving a 2" opening on one side.

12. Trim corners; turn pocket right side out, poke out corners and smooth edges. Turn opening seam allowance to the inside; press flat.

13. Repeat steps 11 and 12 for second pocket.

14. Pin a pocket square to each side of the apron skirt 3½" down from top raw edge and 8" in from each side. *Note: Be sure that the open seam is at the bottom edge of the pocket.*

15. Stitch pockets to apron skirt, stitching close to side and bottom edges. Backstitch at the beginning and end of each seam to secure.

16. Stitch two lines of gathering stitches along the top edge of the skirt ⅛" from edge and close to this line of stitching; gather top edge of skirt to 22" across.

17. Narrowly hem the two long sides of each 3" x 24" tie strip; fold the strips in half along length with right sides together and stitch one end of each tie as shown in Figure 2. Unfold and poke out end to form a point; press.

Figure 2

18. Pleat the other short end of each tie so that it measures a little less than 1½" wide; baste across end to hold pleat in place.

19. Working on the wrong side of each waistband strip, make a mark at the center of each long side and 1" in from each side.

20. With right sides together, stitch one waist tie to each end of one waistband strip; press seams to the wrong side of the waistband strip.

21. Pin the skirt to the right side of the second waistband strip, matching centers and side edges of

skirt to marks 1" in from each side of the waistband as shown in Figure 3.

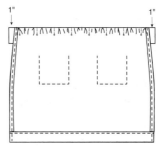

Figure 3

22. Pin the waistband/tie strip to the wrong side of the skirt/waistband section with right sides of waistbands together so skirt is sandwiched between waistband strips.

23. Using a ½" seam allowance on the long edges of the waistband and ¼" across the short edges, stitch waistbands to skirt as shown in Figure 4. *Note: Be careful not to catch the side edges of the ties in your stitching.*

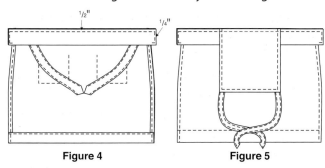

Figure 4   **Figure 5**

24. Before turning, flip this entire section over with the right side of the apron facing up.

25. Center the bib right sides together over skirt/waistband, matching bottom raw edges of bib to top raw edges of skirt as shown in Figure 5.

26. Stitch bib to skirt/waistbands. Turn right side out; press stitched seams carefully, pressing bib up and skirt down. *Note: The waistband will cover 1½" of bottom edge of bib.* Press ½" seam allowance under on remaining waistband edges.

27. Pin top edges of waistband together; topstitch close to all edges of the waistband, catching open edges in your stitching.

28. Press apron thoroughly.

Pot Holder

1. Piece together the leftover scraps from the apron bib and pockets to make an 8½" x 8½" square.

2. Cut a 13½" strip of bias tape; baste the folded strip in place along one diagonal of the square as shown in Figure 6.

Figure 6

3. Layer the lining square wrong side up with the cotton batting on top; place the insulated batting on top of these layers and the scrappy-pieced square on top right side up. Baste layers together.

4. For hanging loop, cut a 5" strip of bias tape. Leaving the piece folded, stitch close to both long edges. Pin this piece over the diagonal strip of bias tape, matching one end to the corner of the square. *Note: One end will be caught when stitching the binding to the front side of the hot pad. The other edge will be flipped over and caught when finishing the back side of the binding.*

5. Open out bias tape and machine-stitch binding right sides together to the front side of the square. Fold binding to the back side and blind-stitch over line of machine stitching. Fold the other end of hanging loop under the back binding edge and catch it in your finishing stitches.

6. To keep the hanging loop together, tack the front and back together just above the corner of the pot holder.

7. Topstitch close to both edges of the diagonal bias tape; remove basting stitches to finish. ❖

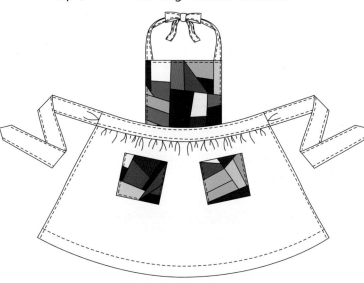

Kitchen Leftovers Apron
Placement Diagram One Size Fits All

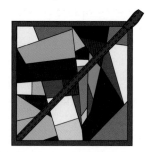

Kitchen Leftovers Pot Holder
Placement Diagram 8½" x 8½"

Garden Snippets

Scraps of pastel florals come together like a bouquet of spring flowers from the garden. The flower appliqués on the place mats are napkin rings.

Project Specifications
Skill Level: Beginner
Coaster Size: 4" x 4"
Place Mat Size: 18" x 13½"
Runner Size: 36" x 13½"

Materials to Make Runner, 2 Place Mats and 6 Coasters
- Assorted pastel floral scraps
- Scrap gold solid
- ⅛ yard pink print
- ⅛ yard muslin
- ¼ yard floral print
- 1⅝ yards green mottled (includes backing)
- 2 pieces batting 19" x 15" for place mats, one 38" x 15" for runner and six 5" x 5" for coasters
- All-purpose thread to match fabrics
- Water-soluble fabric marker
- Basic sewing tools and supplies

Cutting
1. Cut two 15" by fabric width strips green mottled; subcut strips into backing pieces as follows: two 19" x 15" for place mats and one 38" x 15" for runner.

2. Cut six 2¾" by fabric width strips green mottled; subcut strips into two 36½" D, four 9½" C and eight 14" E strips.

3. Cut three 2¼" by fabric width strips green mottled for binding.

4. Cut one 5" by fabric width strip floral print; subcut strip into six 5" squares for coaster backings.

Preparing Flowers
1. Using the flower template given and water-soluble fabric marker, trace five flowers on the wrong side of the pink print leaving ½" between flowers—this traced line will be the stitching line.

2. Place the marked pink print right sides together with the muslin; pin inside each flower to hold in place.

3. Stitch around each flower on traced lines, leaving a 1" opening for turning. ***Note:*** *Try to leave the opening along one of the straighter parts of the flower edges.*

4. Cut out each flower a scant ¼" away from the stitched lines; clip inner curves. Turn flowers right side out; smooth edges.

5. Turn opening seam allowance to the inside; hand-stitch opening closed. Press each flower flat.

6. Topstitch close to the edge on two of the flowers.

7. Using the template given and the water-soluble fabric marker, trace flower centers on the wrong side of the gold solid scrap as for flowers; place the marked scrap right sides together with an unmarked scrap and stitch together on the marked lines.

8. Cut out a scant ¼" around each circle; pull back layer apart from the top layer and clip an X in the back piece as shown in Figure 1. Turn right side out through opening.

Figure 1   **Figure 2**

9. Press circle flat, keeping edges curved; trim backing to within ¼" of stitched edge to reduce bulk as shown in Figure 2.

10. Center a circle in the center of each flower; hand-stitch in place. Machine-stitch close to edges of flower center on the two topstitched flowers to secure layers.

Making Scrappy-Pieced Sections
1. Using the assorted pastel floral scraps, follow the instructions for the scrappy-piecing technique found on page 3. Make enough scrappy-pieced

Garden Snippets Runner
Placement Diagram 36" x 13½"

fabric to cut three 9½" x 9½" A squares and two 9½" x 14" B rectangles. Save the cut-aways for making the coasters.

Runner

1. Join three A squares with four C strips; press seams toward C strips.

2. Sew a D strip to opposite long sides of the pieced unit to complete the runner top; press seams toward D strips.

3. Mark the quilting design given onto the C and D strips referring to the Placement Diagram for positioning.

4. Place the runner-size batting piece on a flat surface; place the runner backing right side up on the batting. Place the stitched runner top right sides together with the backing; pin and stitch layers together all around edges leaving a 4" opening on one side.

5. Clip corners; trim backing and batting even with the edges of the quilt top.

6. Turn runner right side out through opening, poking corners flat. Turn opening edges to the inside as shown in Figure 3; hand-stitch opening closed.

Figure 3   Figure 4

7. Press edges flat. Quilt on marked lines by hand or machine; remove marks.

8. Arrange and pin the three flowers without topstitching on the runner top as desired and referring to the Placement Diagram for suggested placement. When satisfied with placement, stitch flowers in place around flower center, leaving edges of flowers free from stitching as shown in Figure 4.

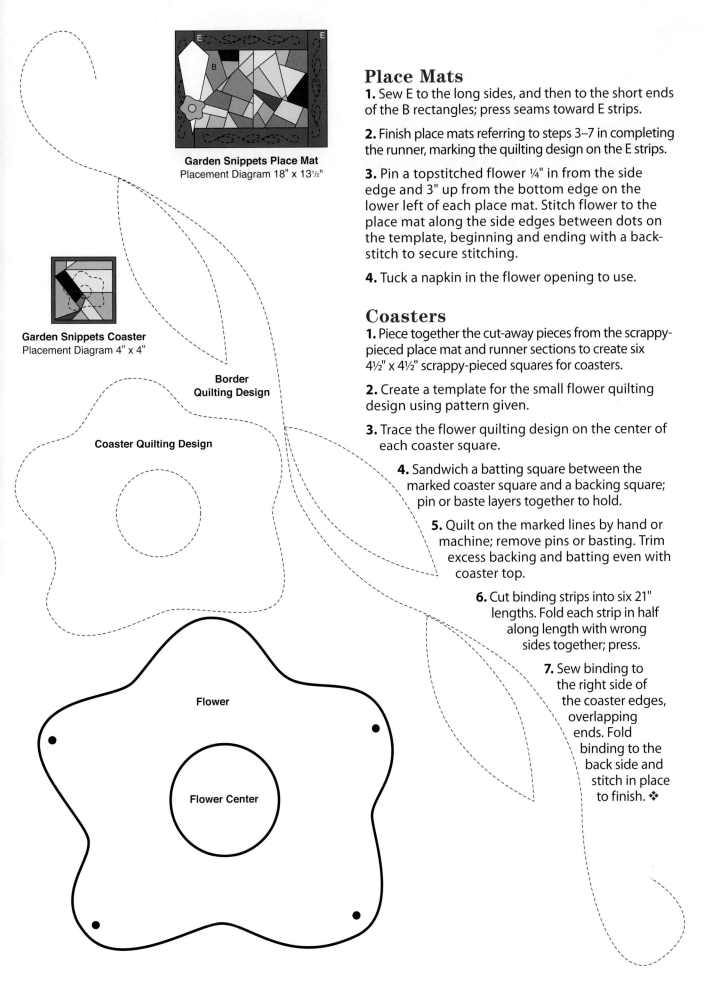

Garden Snippets Place Mat
Placement Diagram 18" x 13½"

Garden Snippets Coaster
Placement Diagram 4" x 4"

Border Quilting Design

Coaster Quilting Design

Flower

Flower Center

Place Mats

1. Sew E to the long sides, and then to the short ends of the B rectangles; press seams toward E strips.

2. Finish place mats referring to steps 3–7 in completing the runner, marking the quilting design on the E strips.

3. Pin a topstitched flower ¼" in from the side edge and 3" up from the bottom edge on the lower left of each place mat. Stitch flower to the place mat along the side edges between dots on the template, beginning and ending with a backstitch to secure stitching.

4. Tuck a napkin in the flower opening to use.

Coasters

1. Piece together the cut-away pieces from the scrappy-pieced place mat and runner sections to create six 4½" x 4½" scrappy-pieced squares for coasters.

2. Create a template for the small flower quilting design using pattern given.

3. Trace the flower quilting design on the center of each coaster square.

4. Sandwich a batting square between the marked coaster square and a backing square; pin or baste layers together to hold.

5. Quilt on the marked lines by hand or machine; remove pins or basting. Trim excess backing and batting even with coaster top.

6. Cut binding strips into six 21" lengths. Fold each strip in half along length with wrong sides together; press.

7. Sew binding to the right side of the coaster edges, overlapping ends. Fold binding to the back side and stitch in place to finish. ❖

Grandmother's Scrap Basket Table Runner

Vintage or reproduction fabric scraps will result in this same look.

Project Specifications
Skill Level: Beginner
Runner Size: 34" x 17"
Block Size: 12" x 12"
Number of Blocks: 2

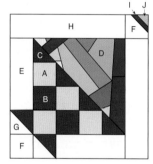

Scrap Basket
12" x 12" Block
Make 2

Materials
- Assorted vintage or reproduction scraps
- 1½" x 8" strip blue solid
- 2½" x 21" strip tan solid
- ½ yard brown mottled
- 1½ yards muslin (includes backing)
- Batting 40" x 23"
- Neutral-color all-purpose thread
- Cream quilting thread
- Basic sewing tools and supplies

Cutting
1. Cut one 18¼" by fabric width strip muslin; subcut strip into one 18¼" K square, two 9⅜" x 9⅜" L squares and two 2⅞" x 2⅞" G squares. Cut the K square on both diagonals to make four K triangles; discard two. Cut the G and L squares in half on one diagonal to make four each L and G triangles.

2. Cut two 2½" by fabric width strips muslin; subcut strips into four 2½" x 10½" H strips, four 2½" x 6½" E strips and four 2½" x 2½" F squares.

3. Cut one 40" x 23" backing piece muslin.

4. Cut three 2¼" by fabric width strips brown mottled for binding.

5. Cut one 2⅞" by fabric width strip brown mottled; subcut strip into six 2⅞" C squares. Cut each C square in half on one diagonal to make 12 C triangles.

6. Trim the remainder of the strip cut in step 5 to 2½" wide; subcut into four 2½" B squares and two 2¼" x 2¼" I squares.

7. Cut eight 2½" x 2½" A squares tan solid.

8. Cut four 1½" x 1½" J squares blue solid.

Making Scrappy-Pieced Sections
1. Using the assorted reproduction scraps, follow the instructions for the scrappy-piecing technique found on page 3. Make enough scrappy-pieced fabric to cut one 8⅞" x 8⅞" square.

2. Cut the square in half on one diagonal to make two D triangles.

Completing the Blocks
1. To complete one Scrap Basket block, join two A squares with one B square and one C triangle as shown in Figure 1; press seams toward B and C.

| **Figure 1** | **Figure 2** | **Figure 3** |

2. Join one each A and B square and one C triangle, again referring to Figure 1; press seams toward B and C.

3. Sew a C triangle to A, again referring to Figure 1; press seam toward C.

4. Arrange and join the pieced rows with one more C triangle to complete the basket triangle base as shown in Figure 2; press seams in one direction.

5. Sew C to G; repeat to make two C-G units.

6. Sew a C-G unit to one end of two E strips to make two C-G-E units as shown in Figure 3; press seams toward the C-G units.

7. Sew one C-G-E unit to one side of the basket triangle base referring to Figure 4; press seam toward the C-G-E unit.

8. Sew an F square to the G end of the remaining C-G-E unit to make a side unit, again referring to Figure 4; press seam toward the G end of the unit.

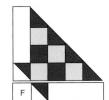

Figure 4

9. Sew the side unit to the remaining short side of the basket triangle unit to complete the basket base.

10. Sew a scrappy-pieced D triangle to the long edge of the basket base; press seam toward D.

11. Mark a diagonal line on the wrong side of each I and J square.

12. Place an I square right sides together on one corner of F and stitch on the marked line as shown in Figure 5; trim seam allowance to ¼" and press I to the right side.

13. Repeat step 12 with J on the F-I unit as shown in Figure 6 to complete one corner unit. Trim seam allowance to ¼"; press J to the right side.

Figure 5

Figure 6

14. Sew an H strip to one E side of the pieced basket unit referring to Figure 7; press seam toward H.

15. Sew the corner unit to one end of another H strip as shown in Figure 8; press seam toward H.

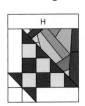

Figure 7

Figure 8

16. Sew the H/corner strip to the remaining D side of the basket unit to complete one Scrap Basket block referring to the block drawing for positioning; press seam toward the H/corner strip.

17. Repeat steps 1–16 to complete a second Scrap Basket block.

Completing the Top

1. Place a marked J square right sides together on the square corner of each K triangle as shown in Figure 9; stitch on the marked line. Trim seam to ¼" and press J to the right side to complete two J-K units, again referring to Figure 9.

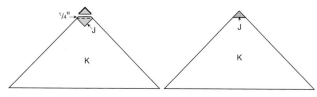

Figure 9

2. Sew L to two adjacent block edges and a J-K unit to one H edge to make one end of the runner as shown in Figure 10; press seams toward L and K. Repeat to make two runner ends.

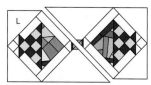

Figure 10

3. Join the two runner ends to complete the top, again referring to Figure 10; press seam in one direction.

Completing the Runner

1. Sandwich the batting between the completed top and prepared backing; pin or baste layers together to hold.

2. Quilt as desired by hand or machine; remove pins or basting. Trim excess backing and batting even with quilt top. *Note: The quilting design given was hand-quilted in each L corner. It was doubled and quilted in each J-K unit.*

3. Join binding strips on short ends with diagonal seams to make one long strip; trim seams to ¼" and press seams open. Fold the strip in half along length with wrong sides together; press.

4. Sew binding to the right side of the runner edges, overlapping ends. Fold binding to the back side and stitch in place to finish. ❖

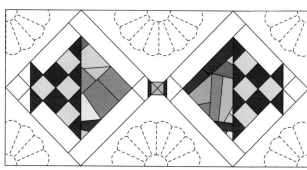

Grandmother's Scrap Basket Table Runner
Placement Diagram 34" x 17"

Quilting Design

Tiny Totes

These little totes are perfect for storing your sewing supplies or your MP3 player, headphones and extra batteries.

Tiny Tote

Project Specifications
Skill Level: Beginner
Tiny Tote Size: 6½" x 5"

Materials
- Scrappy-pieced leftovers measuring 7" x 15½"
- 7½" x 16" lining fabric
- 9" x 6½" for pocket
- Batting 7½" x 16"
- Small amount of polyester fiberfill
- Neutral-color all-purpose thread
- Quilting thread
- Red embroidery floss
- 1 yard matching double-fold wide bias tape
- 3" x 3" square red felt
- 1 heart button
- 1" length 1"-wide hook-and-loop tape or ½" heavy snap
- Water-soluble fabric marker
- Basic sewing tools and supplies

Completing the Tote
1. Sandwich the batting between the scrappy-pieced rectangle and the lining piece; quilt as desired. Trim quilted piece to 6½" x 15".

2. Prepare a template for the curved end using pattern given.

3. Trim one end of the quilted piece using the curved-end template as shown in Figure 1. Mark snap/hook-and-loop tape placement using the water-soluble fabric marker as indicated on template.

Figure 1

4. For pocket, fold the 9" x 6½" piece in half to measure 4½" x 6½" and press.

5. Working on the lining side of the quilted piece, draw a line across the quilted piece, 5⅛" from the straight edge as shown in Figure 2.

Tiny Tote
Placement Diagram 6½" x 5"

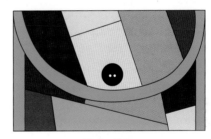

Tinier Tote
Placement Diagram 6½" x 3½"

6. Place the open bottom edges of the pocket piece on the marked line with the folded end toward the straight end of the quilted piece as shown in Figure 3; stitch ¼" from the open bottom edges.

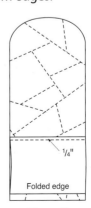

5⅛"

¼"

Folded edge

Figure 2   **Figure 3**

7. Flip the pocket up, over the seam toward the curved edge and baste side edges in place. *Note: The side edges of the pocket should be even with the side edges of the quilted piece.*

8. Stitch down the center of the pocket, creating two smaller pockets as shown in Figure 4.

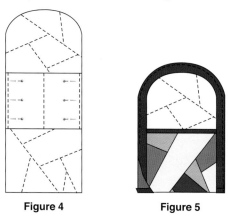

Figure 4   Figure 5

9. Bind short straight end of the quilted pieces using the double-fold wide bias tape.

10. At this point, the quilted piece will naturally fold along the line of stitching created in step 6. Fold the bound end up, matching side edges and enclosing pocket; pin or baste side edges together.

11. Fold the beginning end of the double-fold wide bias tape ¼" to the inside. Place the tape right sides together starting with the folded end at one bottom corner, up along curve, to within 2" of the other bottom corner. Trim tape ¼" longer than needed to finish and fold in as before. Continue stitching to the end for a clean finish as shown Figure 5. Turn tape to the back side; hand-stitch in place to complete binding.

12. Sew a snap or piece of hook-and-loop tape to the tote for closure as indicated on the pattern. Fold the rounded edge over tote opening and mark placement for snap/hook-and-loop tape on straight edge using the water-soluble fabric marker as shown in Figure 6. Sew a button to the front of the tote over the snap or hook-and-loop tape.

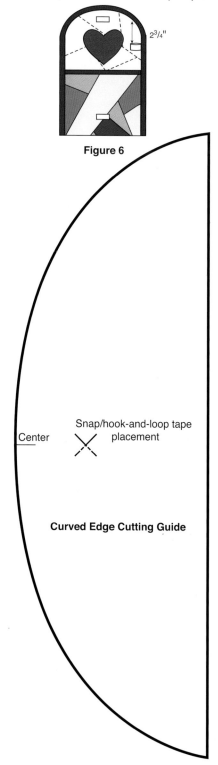

Figure 6

Center

Snap/hook-and-loop tape placement

Curved Edge Cutting Guide

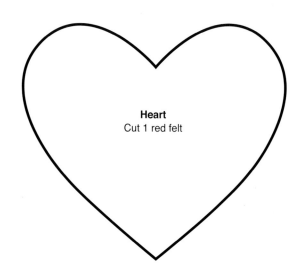

Heart
Cut 1 red felt

13. Prepare a template for the heart shape given; cut one from red felt.

14. Center the heart shape on the inside of the tote flap; stitch it to the flap using 3 strands of red embroidery floss and a buttonhole stitch. Before finishing off the stitching, stuff the heart firmly with polyester batting. Finish stitching and knot off. *Note: If the tote is to be an MP3 tote, eliminate heart and attach a length of braided or rat-tail cord to the sides of the tote for a strap. Make the strap long enough to go over the head and across the body.*

Tinier Tote

Project Specifications
Skill Level: Beginner
Tinier Tote Size: 6½" x 3½"

Materials
- Scrappy-pieced leftovers measuring 7" x 11"
- 7½" x 12" lining fabric
- 6½" x 6½" pocket square
- Batting 7½" x 12"
- Neutral-color all-purpose thread
- Quilting thread
- 1 yard matching double-fold wide bias tape
- 1 (⅝") round black button
- 1" length 1"-wide hook-and-loop tape or ½" heavy snap
- Basic sewing tools and supplies

Completing the Tote
1. Follow the same steps as for the Tiny Tote as follows:

—Trim the quilted piece to 6½" x 10½".

—Fold the pocket square in half to measure 3¼" x 6½".

—Draw the line across the quilted piece 3¾" from the straight edge.

—Instead of stitching down the center of the pocket, create three pockets by stitching 2⅛" in from each side of the tote.

—Attach snap or hook-and-loop tape, centered on curve close to finding and centered approximately 2" down from straight edge. ❖

Tip

If either of these projects will be used as a sewing tote, insert a folded 2½" length of ¼" elastic under the binding on the inside of the curved flap as you sew for a thimble holder. Place the elastic about 2¾" down from the top edge of the curve as shown in Figure 6.

Scrappy Tote Bag

This roomy tote is quick to make when you begin with pre-quilted muslin.

- 2 pieces cotton batting or quilting fleece 1" x 26"
- Neutral-color all-purpose thread
- Water-soluble fabric marker
- Basic sewing tools and supplies

Cutting
1. Cut one 16" x 33½" rectangle pre-quilted muslin.

2. Cut one 16" x 33½" lining piece from muslin.

3. Cut two 3" x 26" handle strips and one 6" x 8½" pocket piece from muslin.

Making Scrappy-Pieced Sections
1. Piece together the leftover scrappy-pieced fabric to make two 6" x 16" rectangles.

Completing the Bag Base
1. Using a water-soluble fabric marker, draw a line 5¼" from each short end on the right side of the pre-quilted muslin piece as shown in Figure 1.

2. With right sides together, align one long edge of a scrappy-pieced strip along one of the lines drawn in step 1 and stitch as shown in Figure 2.

3. Repeat step 2 on the opposite end of the pre-quilted muslin piece; do not trim any fabric away.

4. Flip the scrappy-pieced sections to the right side and press; align side and top edges and baste in place.

5. Serge or zigzag-stitch all edges of the quilted muslin piece, including the layered areas on the ends.

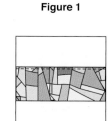

5¼"

Figure 1

Figure 2

Making Handles
1. Press under ¼" on one long edge of each 3" x 26" handle strip; press under another ⅞" on both long edges of each handle strip. *Note: For a really scrappy look, use strips from your box of leftovers for the handles, cutting them to 3" x 26".*

Project Specifications
Skill Level: Beginner
Project Size: 13½" x 14⅜" x 4"

Materials
- Leftovers of scrappy-pieced fabric
- ⅝ yard pre-quilted muslin
- ¾ yard muslin

2. Open pressed edges and insert a 1" x 26" batting strip; fold the long edges over the batting with the ¼" folded edge on top.

3. Stitch close to the ¼" fold and ⅛" away from each side edge.

Making Pocket

1. Fold pocket rectangle in half with right sides together so that the piece measures 6" x 4¼". Stitch along sides and bottom edges, leaving 1½" unsewn for turning as shown in Figure 3.

Figure 3   **Figure 4**

2. Turn pocket; poke out corners. Turn in seam allowances at opening and press.

3. Center pocket 4½" down from one 16" edge of the lining rectangle as shown in Figure 4; stitch in place close to pocket edges.

Completing Bag & Lining

1. Fold the bag in half right sides together along the length so that the piece measures 16" x 16¾".

2. Sew the side seams; lightly press seam allowances open.

3. To make the bag bottom, pull bag front away from bag back at bottom corners. Match side seam of bag to center of bag bottom to form a triangle as shown in Figure 5; pin in place.

4. Draw a line across the triangle 2" from the corner, again referring to Figure 5; stitch on the drawn line. Press flat, but do not trim.

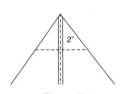

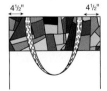

Figure 5   **Figure 6**

5. Repeat steps 1–4 for bag lining, leaving 6" unsewn along one side seam for turning. Press lining seam allowances to one side instead of open.

Attaching Handles

1. With right sides together and raw edges even, pin handles to the top edges of each side of the bag 4½" in from side seams as shown in Figure 6; machine baste in place.

Joining Lining & Bag

1. Turn bag wrong side out, tucking handles down into the inside of the bag.

2. With right sides together, put lining inside the bag; pin together matching side seams and top raw edges.

3. Using a ⅜" seam allowance, stitch bag to lining along top edge; stitch again over first stitching.

4. Turn the bag and lining right side out through the 6" opening; stitch the opening closed.

5. Press both lining and bag flat at seams; tuck lining inside the bag. Press or baste along the top edge; topstitch along the top edge of the bag ⅜" away from the edge.

6. Tack the lining inside the bag at the bottom corners to finish, if desired. ❖

Scrappy Tote Bag
Placement Diagram 13½" x 14⅜" x 4"

Striking!

Bright, fun fabrics contrast with black for a striking combination.

Project Specifications
Skill Level: Beginner
Quilt Size: 50½" x 76"
Block Size: 4" x 4"
Number of Blocks: 4

Materials
- Assorted bright-colored scraps
- 3⅛ yards black solid
- Backing 57" x 82"
- Batting 57" x 82"
- Neutral-color all-purpose thread
- Multicolored quilting thread
- Basic sewing tools and supplies

Corner
4" x 4" Block
Make 4

Cutting

1. Cut seven 2¼" by fabric width strips black solid for binding.

2. Cut six 4½" by fabric width E/H strips black solid.

3. Cut five 9¾" by fabric width strips black solid; subcut strips into (19) 9¾" squares. Cut each square on both diagonals to make 76 C triangles; discard two.

4. Cut one 5⅛" by fabric width strip black solid; subcut strip into six 5⅛" squares. Cut each square in half on one diagonal to make 12 B triangles.

5. Cut one 2⅞" by fabric width strip black solid; subcut strip into eight 2⅞" squares. Cut each square in half on one diagonal to make 16 F triangles.

Making Scrappy-Pieced Sections

1. Using the assorted scraps, follow the instructions for the scrappy-piecing technique found on page 3. Make enough scrappy-pieced fabric to cut (38) 6½" x 6½" A squares, one 7¼" x 7¼" D square and four 3⅜" x 3⅜" G squares.

2. Cut the D square on both diagonals to make four D triangles.

Completing the Top

1. Sew a C triangle to opposite sides of an A square as shown in Figure 1; press seams toward C. Repeat to make 32 A-C units.

X Row
Make 3

Figure 1   **Figure 2**

2. Sew a B triangle to two adjacent sides of an A square as shown in Figure 2; add C to the lower right side, again referring to Figure 2; press seams toward B and C.

3. Join six A-C units as shown in Figure 3; press seams in one direction.

4. Add an A-B-C unit to each end to complete an X row, again referring to Figure 3; press as in step 3.

Figure 3

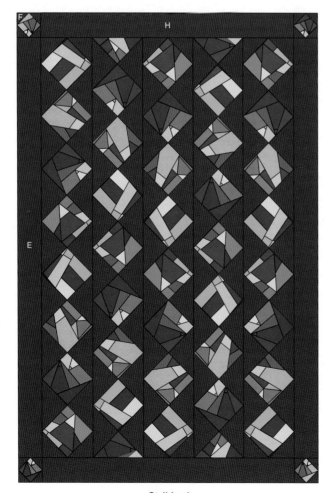

Striking!
Placement Diagram 50½" x 76"

5. Repeat steps 2–4 to complete three X rows.

6. Join one each C and D triangles as shown in Figure 4; press seam toward C. Repeat to make four C-D units.

Figure 4

7. Join seven A-C units with two C-D units to make a Y row as shown in Figure 5; press seams in one direction. Repeat to make two Y rows.

8. Join the X and Y rows referring to the Placement Diagram to complete the pieced center; press seams in one direction.

Completing the Quilt

1. Join the E/H strips on short ends to make one long strip; press seams open. Subcut strip into two 68½" E strips and two 43" H strips.

2. Sew an E strip to opposite long sides of the pieced center; press seams toward E strips.

3. Sew an F triangle to each side of a G

Y Row
Make 2

Figure 5

square to complete a Corner block referring to the block drawing; press seams toward F. Repeat to make four Corner blocks.

4. Sew a Corner block to each end of each G strip; press seams toward G.

5. Sew a corner/G strip to the top and bottom of the pieced center to complete the top; press seams toward strips.

6. Sandwich the batting between the completed top and prepared backing; pin or baste layers together to hold.

7. Quilt as desired by hand or machine; remove pins or basting. Trim excess backing and batting even with quilt top.

8. Join binding strips on short ends with diagonal seams to make one long strip; trim seams to ¼" and press seams open. Fold the strip in half along length with wrong sides together; press.

9. Sew binding to the right side of the quilt edges, overlapping ends. Fold binding to the back side and stitch in place to finish. ❖

Flocking Together

This is a fun wall quilt based on the traditional Birds in the Air pattern. Half of the block is a scrappy-pieced nest, complete with babies, and the other half is made of triangle "birds."

Project Notes

Before you begin this project, you need to decide on the "bird families." Will you have two adult birds and babies in the nest? Will you have a single mom with babies in the nest? Will you have a single adult? Will you have three grown birds flying home to nest?

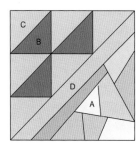

Bird's Nest
10" x 10" Block
Make 9

The basic block is shown in the block drawing. Refer to the Placement Diagram to see the different-size families. The instructions given are to complete the quilt as shown. Your quilt could be totally different.

Project Specifications

Skill Level: Intermediate
Project Size: 34½" x 37"
Block Size: 10" x 10"
Number of Blocks: 9

Materials

- Variety of scraps in bird's nest colors—beiges, light greens, light browns, cream, tans
- Dark brown scraps for worms
- 9 different blue fat quarters
- ⅛ yard square gold pin dot
- ¼ yard green mottled
- ⅝ yard brown mottled
- 1¼ yards light blue solid
- Batting 41" x 43"
- Backing 41" x 43"
- Neutral-color and green all-purpose thread
- Quilting thread
- Water-soluble fabric marker
- Basic sewing tools and supplies

Cutting

1. Cut one 3⅞" x 10" strip from each blue fat quarter; subcut strips into two 3⅞" squares.

Cut each square in half on one diagonal to make four B triangles each fabric.

2. Cut 11 total 1½" x 2½" O pieces from blue prints for baby birds.

3. Cut three 3⅞" by fabric width strips light blue solid; subcut strips into (25) 3⅞" squares. Cut each square in half on one diagonal to make 50 C triangles. Discard one triangle.

4. Cut five 1½" by fabric width strips light blue solid; subcut strips into nine 15" D strips.

5. Cut one 3½" by fabric width strip light blue solid; subcut strip into seven 3½" E squares, one 4½" I rectangle, one 2" P rectangle, one 2" x 2" K square and one 2" x 4" Q rectangle.

6. Cut one 10½" by fabric width strip light blue solid; subcut strip into six 2½" G strips, two 3½" J strips and nine 1½" F strips.

7. Cut two 2¼" by fabric width strips light blue solid for binding.

8. Cut three 2" by fabric width L/M/R strips brown mottled.

9. Cut three 1½" by fabric width strips brown mottled; subcut strips into nine 11" H strips.

10. Cut two 2¼" by fabric width strips brown mottled for binding.

11. Cut six 2" x 2" N squares gold pin dot for beaks.

Making Scrappy-Pieced Sections

1. Using your chosen scraps and referring to the scrappy-piecing technique on page 3, make enough scrappy-pieced fabric to cut five 8⅜" x 8⅜" squares.

2. Cut each square in half on one diagonal to make 10 A triangles. Set aside one triangle for another project.

Completing the Blocks

1. Sew B to C along the diagonal to make one B-C unit; press seam toward B. Repeat to make 23 B-C units.

2. To complete one Bird's Nest block, center and sew a D strip to the longest edge of an A triangle; trim extra at each end at the same angle as A as shown in Figure 1.

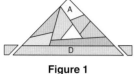

Figure 1   **Figure 2**

3. Join three B-C units with C in rows and join the rows to make a block corner as shown in Figure 2; press seams in adjoining rows in opposite directions. **Note:** *Refer to the Placement Diagram to see the different variations on the number of B-C units used in the various blocks.*

4. Sew the block corner to the A-D unit to complete one block referring to the block drawing.

5. To add baby-bird beaks to the blocks, fold each N square on one diagonal; press and bring the two folded corners down to the middle of the open bottom edge to make a prairie point for beak as shown in Figure 3; press. Repeat to make six beaks.

6. Before stitching D to A, pin a beak with the folded side against A as shown in Figure 4; baste in place. **Note:** *The location of each beak is determined*

by the number of beaks and/or baby birds in the block. Start the first piece in the center and work out evenly to the edges, aligning edges of beaks with the edge of A, not overlapping as shown in Figure 5. Sew D to A and add a block corner unit to complete a block with baby-bird beaks as in steps 2–4.

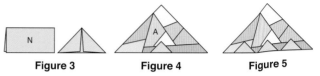

Figure 3   **Figure 4**   **Figure 5**

7. To make baby birds, fold an O rectangle in half with right sides together along the 2½" side; stitch along one side adjacent to the fold as shown in Figure 6. Turn right side out, center the seam and press to complete one baby bird as shown in Figure 7. Repeat to make 11 baby birds.

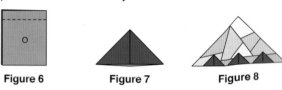

Figure 6   **Figure 7**   **Figure 8**

8. Place the baby birds against A as desired with the seam side up as shown in Figure 8. Add a D strip and a block corner unit to complete a block with baby birds.

9. Repeat steps 2–4 to complete nine blocks, inserting beaks and baby birds as desired or as shown in the Placement Diagram.

Completing the Top

1. Turn one block over and working in the bottom right corner (as you are looking at the block), mark a dot ¼" in from each side of the block where the side and bottom seam allowances cross using the water-soluble fabric marker.

2. Turn the block right side up and pin an F strip to the left side of the block, pinning the strip so that the top edges are even and the excess hangs off the bottom edge of the block. Stitch strip to the block, stopping stitching at the marked dot as shown in Figure 9; press seam toward F.

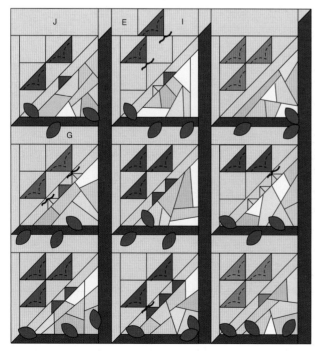

Flocking Together
Placement Diagram 34½" x 37"

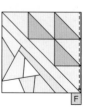

Figure 9

3. Pin an H strip to the bottom of the block pinning strip so that the right-hand side edges are even and the excess hangs off the left-hand side of the block as shown in Figure 10. *Note: Do not stretch the A edge.*

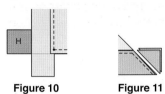

Figure 10   Figure 11

4. Stitch strip to the block, stopping stitching at the marked dot; press seam toward H.

5. Using the excess fabric at the bottom left corner of the block, miter the corner, stitching from the dot to the outside edge at a 45-degree angle as shown in Figure 11; trim seam to ¼". Press seam open.

6. Repeat steps 1–5 with all blocks.

7. Arrange the blocks in vertical rows to determine arrangement. Sew J to the top edge of the top blocks in the two outside rows; press seams toward J.

8. Sew the remaining B-C unit between E and I pieces as shown in Figure 12; press seams toward E and I. Sew this strip to the top edge of the top block in the center row; press seam toward the pieced strip.

Figure 12

9. Sew G to the top edge of the remaining blocks; press seams toward G.

10. Join the blocks to make the rows as arranged; press seams in one direction.

11. Place a P piece right sides together on one end of L as shown in Figure 13; stitch a diagonal seam, again referring to Figure 13. Trim seam to ¼"; press seam open. Trim excess from the brown end of the strip to complete the 37½"-long L-P strip.

12. Repeat step 11 with K and M to make a K-M strip and with Q and R to make a Q-R strip, again referring to Figure 13. Trim excess from the brown end of each strip to complete the 37½"-long K-M and Q-R strips.

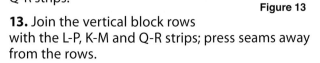

Figure 13

13. Join the vertical block rows with the L-P, K-M and Q-R strips; press seams away from the rows.

14. Prepare a template for the leaf piece using pattern given. Cut as directed on pattern, adding a ⅛"–¼" seam allowance all around for hand appliqué.

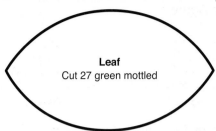

Leaf
Cut 27 green mottled

15. Arrange and appliqué leaves in place as desired or as shown in the Placement Diagram to complete the top.

Completing the Quilt

1. Mark the wing quilting pattern given on each B piece using water-soluble fabric marker.

Wing Quilting Pattern

2. Sandwich the batting between the completed top and prepared backing; pin or baste layers together to hold.

3. Quilt as desired and on marked lines by hand or machine; remove pins or basting. Trim excess backing and batting even with quilt top.

4. Join the light blue solid binding strips on short ends with diagonal seams to make one long strip; trim seams to ¼" and press seams open. Fold the strip in half along length with wrong sides together; press.

5. Sew the light blue binding to the right side of the light blue quilt edges, beginning ¼" from one blue/brown corner and ending ¼" from the opposite blue/brown corner and leaving excess at each end of the binding.

6. Repeat steps 4 and 5 with the brown binding strips on the brown edges.

7. Miter the binding ends at each corner in the same way as for the F-H corners.

8. Cut very narrow strips dark brown scraps on the straight grain of the fabric to make "worms."

9. Curl the worm strips as you do ribbon; find the center of each worm and hand-tack in place at the tip of the B-C units as if the mother birds are bringing worms to the babies to finish. ❖

Association Meeting

Use the leftover fabrics from the Flocking Together project to make this cute companion wall hanging.

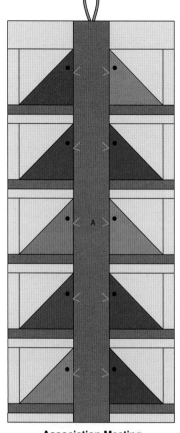

Association Meeting
Placement Diagram 9¼" x 22⅛"

Project Specifications
Skill Level: Beginner
Project Size: 9¼" x 22⅛"

Materials
• 5 different 3⅞" x 3⅞" B squares blue prints
• ¼ yard light blue solid
• ¼ yard brown wood-grain print
• Batting 10" x 23"
• Backing 10" x 23"
• Neutral-color all-purpose thread
• Quilting thread
• Orange embroidery floss
• Water-soluble fabric marker
• 4" length of jute
• 10 (3mm) black beads
• Basic sewing tools and supplies

Cutting
1. Cut one 3⅞" by fabric width strip light blue solid; subcut strip into five 3⅞" squares and two 2" x 4⅛" F strips. Cut each square in half on one diagonal to make 10 C triangles.

2. Cut two 1⅛" by fabric width strips light blue solid; subcut strips into (10) 3½" D strips and (10) 4⅛" E strips.

3. Cut one 2½" x 24" A strip brown wood-grain print.

4. Cut one 1" by fabric width strip brown wood-grain print; subcut strip into (10) 4⅛" G strips.

Completing the Top
1. Sew B to C along the diagonal to make a B-C unit; press seam toward B. Repeat to make 10 B-C units.

2. Sew a D strip to the C side and an E strip to the top edge of C as shown in Figure 1; press seams toward D and E strips. Repeat to make eight B-C-D-E units.

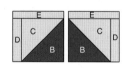

Figure 1   Figure 2

3. Sew a D strip to the C side and an F strip to the top edge of C to complete a B-C-D-F unit as shown in Figure 2; press seams toward D and F strips. Repeat to make two B-C-D-F units.

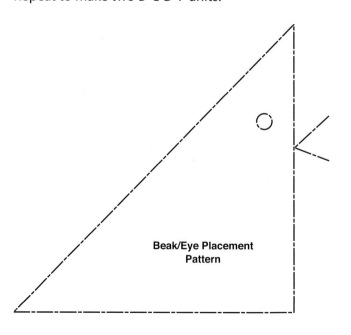

Beak/Eye Placement Pattern

4. Sew a G strip to the B side of each pieced unit as shown in Figure 3; press seams toward G strips.

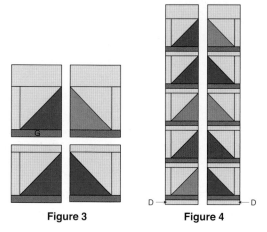

Figure 3   Figure 4

5. Join four B-C-D-E units to make a strip as shown in Figure 4; press seams toward G strips. Repeat to make two strips.

6. Sew a B-C-D-F unit to the top and a D piece to the bottom of each strip; press seams toward G and D strips, again referring to Figure 4.

7. Join the two pieced strips with A to complete the pieced top referring to the Placement Diagram for positioning; press seams toward A strip.

Completing the Quilt

1. Place the batting piece on a flat surface; place the stitched backing right side up on the batting. Fold the 4" length of jute and center on the top edge of the backing as shown in Figure 5. Place the pieced top right sides together with the backing top; pin and stitch layers together all around edges leaving a 4" opening on one side. *Note: A narrow sleeve for hanging may be added here, if desired.*

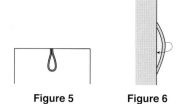

Figure 5   Figure 6

2. Clip corners; trim backing and batting even with the edges of the quilt top.

3. Turn project right side out through opening, poking corners flat. Turn opening edges to the inside as shown in Figure 6; hand-stitch opening closed.

4. Press edges flat. Quilt as desired by hand or machine.

5. Using the beak/eye pattern, mark the position of the bead on B and the beak design on A using a water-erasable fabric marker.

6. Stitch a bead to each B piece as marked.

7. Using 3 strands of orange embroidery floss, straight-stitch a beak on A as marked.

8. Remove marks to complete the project.

9. Hang using jute hanging loop. ❖

Joy!

A neutral-color scrappy-pieced background is the perfect place for these bunnies to run and leap for Joy!

Project Specifications
Skill Level: Beginner
Quilt Size: 50" x 50"

Materials
- Assorted large neutral-color scraps
- Scrap yellow solid
- ⅛ yard pink mottled
- ⅓ yard light green solid
- ⅝ yard brown mottled
- 1½ yards cream print
- Batting 56" x 56"
- All-purpose thread to match fabrics
- Water-soluble fabric marker
- Basic sewing tools and supplies

Cutting
1. Cut four 2" by fabric width strips light green solid; subcut strips into (28) 4" C rectangles, nine 2" E squares and four 2¾" H rectangles.

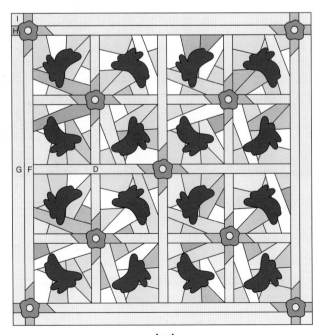

Joy!
Placement Diagram 50" x 50"

2. Cut five 2" x 43" strips along the length of the cream print; subcut strips into (16) 8" B strips, four 19" D strips and four 39" F strips.

3. Cut four 2¾" x 43" G strips along the length of the cream print.

4. Cut five 2¼" by fabric width strips along the length of the cream print for binding.

5. Prepare templates for appliqué pieces; cut as directed, adding a ⅛"–¼" seam allowance for hand appliqué.

6. Transfer registration line from pattern to each rabbit using the water-soluble fabric marker.

Making Scrappy-Pieced Sections
1. Using the assorted scraps, follow the instructions for the scrappy-piecing technique found on page 3. Make enough scrappy-pieced fabric to cut (16) 10" x 10" A squares.

Preparing Sashing Strips
1. Make a mark on the wrong side of each C rectangle 2" from one corner as shown in Figure 1; draw a diagonal line from the mark to the opposite corner, again referring to Figure 1.

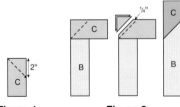

Figure 1   **Figure 2**

2. Place a C piece right sides together with a B piece as shown in Figure 2; stitch on the marked line, again referring to Figure 2.

3. Trim seam to ¼"; press C to the right side to complete a B-C strip, again referring to Figure 2.

4. Repeat steps 2 and 3 to complete 16 B-C strips.

5. Repeat steps 2 and 3 with C and D to complete four C-D strips.

Completing the Top

1. Join two A squares with one B-C strip to make a two-block row as shown in Figure 3; press seams toward the B-C strip. Repeat to make a second two-block row.

Figure 3   **Figure 4**

2. Join two B-C strips with an E square to complete a B-C-E sashing row as shown in Figure 4; press seams toward E. Repeat to make four B-C-E sashing rows.

3. Join the two-block row with a B-C-E sashing row to complete one quilt quarter as shown in Figure 5; press seams toward the sashing row.

Figure 5   **Figure 6**

4. Mark a diagonal line on each A square using the water-soluble marker and referring to Figure 6.

5. Position a rabbit shape 1" from the corner on the marked diagonal lines on each A square using the registration marks on the rabbit and Figure 7 as guides for placement; hand-appliqué the shapes in place.

Figure 7   **Figure 8**

6. Center and hand-appliqué a flower center to a flower. Center and hand-appliqué a flower unit to E to complete one four-block unit as shown in Figure 8.

7. Repeat steps 1–6 to complete four four-block units.

8. Join two four-block units with a C-D strip to make a row; press seams toward the C-D strip. Repeat to make two rows.

9. Join the remaining C-D strips with E; press seams toward the C-D strips.

10. Join the two rows with the C-D-E strip; press seams toward the C-D-E strips.

11. Center and hand-appliqué a flower unit on the center E to complete the pieced center.

Completing the Quilt

1. Sew C to each end of each F strip as in Preparing Sashing Strips to complete four C-F strips.

2. Sew a C-F strip to opposite sides of the pieced center; press seams toward C-F strips.

3. Sew an E square to each end of each of the remaining C-F strips; press seams away from E.

4. Sew a C-F-E strip to the remaining sides of the pieced center; press seams toward the strips.

5. Sew an H rectangle to each end of each G strip; press seams toward G.

6. Sew a G-H strip to opposite sides of the pieced center; press seams toward the G-H strips.

7. Sew an I square to each end of each remaining G-H strip; press seams away from I.

8. Sew the G-H-I strips to the remaining sides of the pieced center; press seams toward the G-H-I strips.

9. Center and hand-appliqué a flower unit on the corner E squares to complete the top.

10. Sandwich the batting between the completed top and prepared backing; pin or baste layers together to hold.

11. Quilt as desired by hand or machine; remove pins or basting. Trim excess backing and batting even with quilt top.

12. Join binding strips on short ends with diagonal seams to make one long strip; trim seams to ¼" and press seams open. Fold the strip in half along length with wrong sides together; press.

13. Sew binding to the right side of the quilt edges, overlapping ends. Fold binding to the back side and stitch in place to finish. ❖

Flower
Cut 9 pink mottled

Flower Center
Cut 9 yellow solid

Rabbit
Cut 16 brown mottled

Little Leftovers

Use your leftovers to make these useful items for your quilting friends.

Project Specifications
Skill Level: Beginner
Pincushion: 4½" x 4½"
Scissors Case Size: 3¼" x 6½"

Materials
- Assorted scraps
- 8" x 8" square cream solid for scissors lining case
- 5" x 5" square navy corduroy for pincushion backing
- 2" x 4" piece red wool felt
- Batting 8" x 8"
- Neutral-color all-purpose thread
- Red and ecru pearl cotton
- Polyester fiberfill
- ¾" red round button
- ⅝" blue square button
- Small amount of steel wool
- Basic sewing tools and supplies

Pincushion

Making Scrappy-Pieced Section
1. Using the assorted scraps, follow the instructions for the scrappy-piecing technique found on page 3 to make a 5" x 5" A square.

Completing the Pincushion
1. Layer the A square right sides together with backing piece; stitch all around, leaving a 2" opening for turning.

2. Turn right side out through the opening; poke out corners and smooth edges.

3. Stuff firmly; turn in seam allowance and hand-stitch opening closed.

4. Thread a needle with an 18" length of red pearl cotton. Find the center of the stuffed pincushion. Using a double thread, insert the needle through the backing fabric and come out on the top center of the pincushion—do not pull the thread all the way through, as shown in Figure 1. Bring the needle up through one hole of the ¾" red round button and down through the other hole. Take

the needle back through the pincushion about ⅛" away from where it came up.

Figure 1

5. Tie the ends of the pearl cotton together on the back side of the pincushion; knot securely. Tie ends into a small bow and trim.

6. Make a template for the small heart; cut two from red wool felt.

7. Layer the two hearts and buttonhole-stitch around the outer edges, stuffing heart with a small bit of steel wool. **Note:** *Steel wool is used to sharpen needles.*

8. Cut a 4" length of red pearl cotton; thread it through the top center edge of the heart and knot it so that it can be looped around the button of the pincushion to finish.

Scissors Case

Making Scrappy-Pieced Section
1. Using the assorted scraps, follow the instructions for the scrappy-piecing technique found on page 3 to make an 8" x 8" square.

Completing the Scissors Case
1. Prepare a template for the scissors case using the pattern given.

2. Trace the template shape on the wrong side of the patchwork piece.

3. Layer thin batting with lining piece right side up, and scrappy-pieced fabric wrong side up; stitch the layers together along the traced line, beginning on the straight edge and leaving 2" unsewn for turning.

4. Trim a ¼" seam allowance all around. Clip off bottom point and into the inner point where curves meet.

5. Turn right side out through opening, poking out bottom point and smoothing curves; press lightly. Turn in seam allowance at opening; hand-stitch closed. Machine-stitch along the centerline of the case as marked on pattern.

6. Using the ecru pearl cotton, blanket-stitch along the top curves of the scissors case referring to the photo.

7. Fold the scissors case in half along the stitched centerline. Pin straight edges together. Using ecru pearl cotton, blanket-stitch along the open straight edges of the scissors case to hold front and back layers together.

8. Fold one curved edge down and tack in place with the blue square button to finish. ❖

Tips

For the embellishments, dig through your collection of bias tape, ribbons and buttons. This is a good time to use up the odds and ends you find there.

Be sure to add a label to the back of your completed quilt project.

Pincushion
Placement Diagram 4½" x 4½"

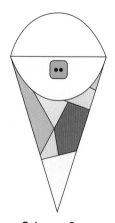

Scissors Case
Placement Diagram 3¼" x 6½"

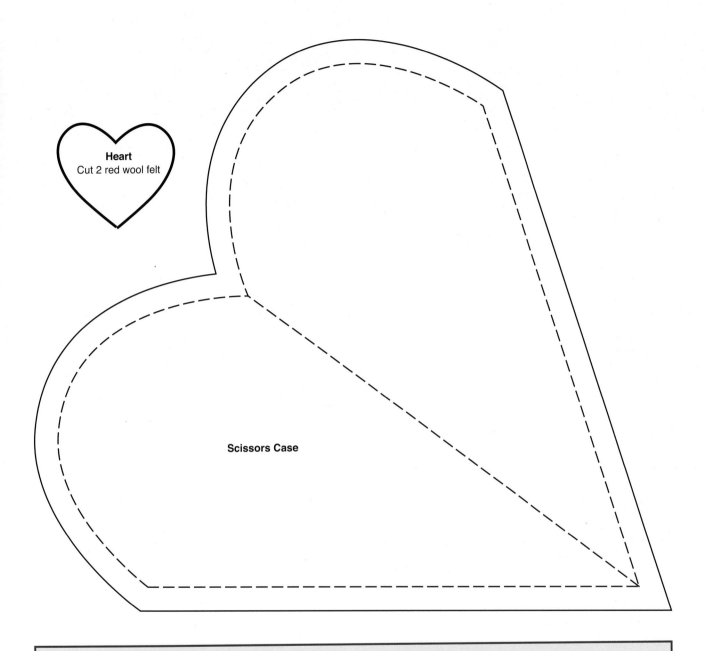

Heart
Cut 2 red wool felt

Scissors Case

Snow Scene Chowder
My all-time favorite way to use leftover turkey or chicken is in this delicious soup.

Ingredients
- 1 chicken bouillon cube
- 2 cups boiling water
- 2 cups diced potatoes
- ½ cup sliced carrots
- ½ cup sliced celery
- ¼ cup chopped onion
- 1½ tsp. salt
- ¼ tsp. pepper
- ¼ cup margarine
- ¼ cup flour
- 2 cups milk
- 2 cups shredded cheddar cheese
- 1 cup diced cooked chicken or turkey

Dissolve bouillon cube in water; add vegetables and seasonings. Cover; simmer 10 minutes. Do not drain. Make a white sauce with margarine, flour and milk. Add cheese; stir until melted. Add chicken and undrained vegetables. Heat; do not boil. Makes 6–8 servings.

Scraps Squared Nursing Cover

Whether it's a nursing cover, a wall quilt or a larger-size quilt, this is the perfect project for using your small scraps.

Project Specifications
Skill Level: Beginner
Project Size: 34" x 27"

Materials
- Variety of scraps, 6" square or smaller of all shapes and colors
- ¼ yard red tonal
- ½ yard muslin
- 1¼ yards tan solid
- Batting 40" x 33" and 2" x 26" strip
- Backing 40" x 33"
- Neutral-color all-purpose thread
- Quilting thread
- 17 (¼") red buttons
- 2 (⅞") red buttons
- 8" hook-and-loop tape
- Basic sewing tools and supplies

Cutting
1. Cut three 2¼" by fabric width strips tan solid for binding.

2. Cut four 2½" by fabric width strips tan solid; subcut strips into two 23½" J strips and two 34½" K strips.

3. Cut two 4¾" by fabric width strips tan solid; subcut strips into (13) 4¾" squares. Set aside four of these squares for E. Cut the remaining nine squares on both diagonals to make 36 B triangles as shown in Figure 1.

Figure 1

4. Cut one 6" x 26½" L strip tan solid for neck strap.

5. Cut two 4¾" by fabric width strips muslin; subcut strips into nine 4¾" squares. Cut each square on both diagonals to make 36 A triangles, again referring to Figure 1.

6. Cut one 2⅝" by fabric width strip muslin; subcut strip into (16) 2⅝" F squares.

7. Cut four 1½" by fabric width strips red tonal; subcut strips into two 21½" H strips and two 30½" I strips.

Making Scrappy-Pieced Sections
1. Using your chosen scraps and referring to the scrappy-piecing technique on page 3, make enough scrappy-pieced fabric to cut the following: (18) 4" x 4" C squares, (10) 4" x 2¼" D rectangles and four 2¼" x 2¼" G squares.

Making Setting Squares
1. Place an A triangle right sides together with a B triangle; stitch along one short side as shown in Figure 2. Press seam toward B. Repeat to make two A-B units.

Figure 2   **Figure 3**

2. Join the two A-B units as shown in Figure 3 to complete one setting unit; press seam in one direction.

3. Repeat steps 1 and 2 to complete 17 setting units; trim each unit to 4" x 4" square, if necessary.

Making Flying Geese Units
1. Draw a diagonal line from corner to corner on the wrong side of each F square.

2. Layer two F squares on one E square with right sides together as shown in Figure 4. *Note: The points of the F squares will overlap slightly.* Trim the points where they overlap as shown in Figure 5.

Figure 4   **Figure 5**

3. Stitch ¼" away from both sides of the marked lines on each piece as shown in Figure 6.

1/4"

Figure 6   **Figure 7**

4. Cut apart on the marked lines as shown in Figure 7; press seams toward E.

5. Lay another F square right sides together on the corner of each of the E-F units as shown in Figure 8; stitch ¼" on both sides of the marked line, again referring to Figure 8.

1/4"

Figure 8

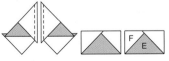

Figure 9

6. Cut the stitched E-F units apart on the marked lines to complete two E-F flying geese units as shown in Figure 9; press seams toward E.

7. Repeat steps 2–6 to make three more sets to total 16 E-F units; set aside two units for another project.

Completing the Top

1. Join two G squares, three D rectangles and four E-F units to make the top row as shown in Figure 10;

press seams away from E-F units. Repeat to make the bottom row.

Figure 10

2. Join two E-F units with three A-B units and four C squares to make an X row as shown in Figure 11; press seams toward C squares. Repeat to make three X rows.

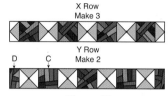

Figure 11

3. Join two D rectangles with three C squares and four A-B units to make a Y row, again referring to Figure 11; press seams toward C squares. Repeat to make two Y rows.

4. Join the rows to complete the pieced center referring to the Placement Diagram for positioning; press seams in one direction.

5. Sew an H strip to opposite sides and I strips to the top and bottom of the pieced center; press seams toward H and I strips.

6. Sew a J strip to opposite sides and K strips to the top and bottom of the pieced center; press seams toward J and K strips to complete the pieced top.

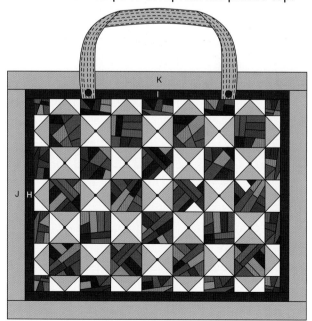

Scraps Squared Nursing Cover
Placement Diagram 34" x 27"

Completing the Quilt

1. Sandwich the batting between the completed top and prepared backing; pin or baste layers together to hold.

2. Quilt as desired by hand or machine; remove pins or basting. Trim excess backing and batting even with quilt top.

3. Join binding strips on short ends with diagonal seams to make one long strip; trim seams to ¼" and press seams open. Fold the strip in half along length with wrong sides together; press.

4. Sew binding to the right side of the quilt edges, overlapping ends. Fold binding to the back side and stitch in place

5. Sew a ¼" button in the center of each A-B unit.

Adding the Neck Strap

1. Press under ¼" on each short end of L; press under 2" on one long edge of L. Press under ½" on the remaining long edge of L. Turn that edge in another 1½" and press.

2. Open out the pressed L strip; lay the 2" x 26" strip of batting inside, inserting the batting ends under the folds at the ends of the L strip. Fold the edges of the strip again with the 1½"-wide folded edge on top.

3. Stitch close to all folded edges, down the center of the strap and adding one more line of stitching between the center and the outer edge to end up with five rows of stitching along length as shown in Figure 12. Stitch close to each end.

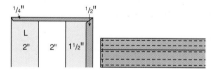

Figure 12

4. Cut four pieces of hook tape 1¾" long; sew these pieces to the ends of the strap with two pieces at each end to make it adjustable. Place one piece ¼" from the end of the strap and the other 1½" from the end of the strap; stitch in place all around each piece.

5. Sew a ⅞" button over the hook tape at the end of the strap.

6. Cut two pieces of loop tape 1¾" long. Sew each loop piece to the quilt top 1" from the top edge and 8" or 9" in from each side edge to finish. ***Note: The length of the strap and the placement of the hook-and-loop tape is adjustable as necessary for the nursing mother.***

Other Size Options

If you have lots of scraps to use up, you might want to make a larger quilt. A small baby quilt could be made using 6½" (unfinished size) scrappy squares. A nap quilt could be made using 8½" (unfinished size) scrappy squares. Larger-size scraps should be used for larger quilts. materials and cutting instructions follow for those options.

Small Baby Quilt (quilt not shown)
Size: 44" x 56"

Materials
- Variety of scraps of all shapes and sizes
- ⅜ yard red tonal
- ¾ yard muslin
- 1⅝ yards tan solid
- Batting 50" x 62"
- Backing 50" x 62"
- OMIT buttons for a baby quilt

Instructions
1. Cut six 2¼" by fabric width binding strips tan solid.

2. Cut five 3" by fabric width J/K strips tan solid (piece and cut as necessary).

3. Cut three 7¼" by fabric width strips tan solid; subcut strips into nine 7¼" B and four 7¼" E squares. Cut each B square on both diagonals to make 36 B triangles.

4. Cut two 7¼" by fabric width strips muslin; subcut strips into nine 7¼" A squares. Cut each square on both diagonals to make 36 A triangles.

5. Cut two 3⅞" by fabric width strips muslin; subcut strips into (16) 3⅞" F squares.

6. Cut five 2" by fabric width H/I strips red tonal (piece and cut as necessary).

7. Cut (18) 6½" x 6½" C squares scrappy-pieced units.

8. Cut (10) 3½" x 6½" D rectangles scrappy-pieced units.

9. Cut four 3½" x 3½" G squares scrappy-pieced units.

10. Refer to instructions for the Nursing Cover to complete the quilt.

Nap Quilt (quilt not shown)
Size: 58" x 74"

Materials
- Variety of scraps of all shapes and sizes
- ⅝ yard red tonal
- 1¼ yards muslin
- 2⅓ yards tan solid
- Batting 64" x 80"
- Backing 64" x 80"
- OMIT buttons for a child's quilt

Instructions
1. Cut seven 2¼" by fabric width binding strips tan solid.

2. Cut seven 3½" by fabric width J/K strips tan solid (piece and cut as necessary).

3. Cut four 9¼" by fabric width strips tan solid; subcut strips into nine 9¼" B and four 9¼" E squares. Cut each B square on both diagonals to make 36 B triangles.

4. Cut three 9¼" by fabric width strips muslin; subcut strips into nine 9¼" A squares. Cut each square on both diagonals to make 36 A triangles.

5. Cut two 4⅞" by fabric width strips muslin; subcut strips into (16) 4⅞" F squares.

6. Cut six 2½" by fabric width H/I strips red tonal (piece and cut as necessary).

7. Cut (18) 8½" x 8½" C squares scrappy-pieced units.

8. Cut (10) 4½" x 8½" D rectangles scrappy-pieced units.

9. Cut four 4½" x 4½" G squares scrappy-pieced units.

10. Refer to instructions for the Nursing Cover to complete the quilt. ❖

Fabrics & Supplies

Page 5, Now Starring: Leftovers
Machine-quilted by Jessica Brunnemer.

Page 14, Casserole Carrier
Warm & Natural cotton batting and Insul-Bright insulated batting from The Warm Company, and Luxite® Bone Rings.

Page 16, Kitchen Leftovers
Warm & Natural cotton batting and Insul-Bright batting from The Warm Company.

Page 25, Tiny Totes
Warm & Natural cotton batting from The Warm Company.

Page 30, Striking!
Machine-quilted by Nancy Watson.

Metric Conversion Charts

Metric Conversions

Canada/U.S. Measurement		Multiplied by		Metric Measurement
yards	x	.9144	=	metres (m)
yards	x	91.44	=	centimetres (cm)
inches	x	2.54	=	centimetres (cm)
inches	x	25.40	=	millimetres (mm)
inches	x	.0254	=	metres (m)

Canada/U.S. Measurement		Multiplied by		Metric Measurement
centimetres	x	.3937	=	inches
metres	x	1.0936	=	yards

Standard Equivalents

Canada/U.S. Measurement		Metric Measurement		
⅛ inch	=	3.20 mm	=	0.32 cm
¼ inch	=	6.35 mm	=	0.635 cm
⅜ inch	=	9.50 mm	=	0.95 cm
½ inch	=	12.70 mm	=	1.27 cm
⅝ inch	=	15.90 mm	=	1.59 cm
¾ inch	=	19.10 mm	=	1.91 cm
⅞ inch	=	22.20 mm	=	2.22 cm
1 inch	=	25.40 mm	=	2.54 cm
⅛ yard	=	11.43 cm	=	0.11 m
¼ yard	=	22.86 cm	=	0.23 m
⅜ yard	=	34.29 cm	=	0.34 m
½ yard	=	45.72 cm	=	0.46 m
⅝ yard	=	57.15 cm	=	0.57 m
¾ yard	=	68.58 cm	=	0.69 m
⅞ yard	=	80.00 cm	=	0.80 m
1 yard	=	91.44 cm	=	0.91 m
1⅛ yards	=	102.87 cm	=	1.03 m
1¼ yards	=	114.30 cm	=	1.14 m

Canada/U.S. Measurement		Metric Measurement		Metric Measurement
1⅜ yards	=	125.73 cm	=	1.26 m
1½ yards	=	137.16 cm	=	1.37 m
1⅝ yards	=	148.59 cm	=	1.49 m
1¾ yards	=	160.02 cm	=	1.60 m
1⅞ yards	=	171.44 cm	=	1.71 m
2 yards	=	182.88 cm	=	1.83 m
2⅛ yards	=	194.31 cm	=	1.94 m
2¼ yards	=	205.74 cm	=	2.06 m
2⅜ yards	=	217.17 cm	=	2.17 m
2½ yards	=	228.60 cm	=	2.29 m
2⅝ yards	=	240.03 cm	=	2.40 m
2¾ yards	=	251.46 cm	=	2.51 m
2⅞ yards	=	262.88 cm	=	2.63 m
3 yards	=	274.32 cm	=	2.74 m
3⅛ yards	=	285.75 cm	=	2.86 m
3¼ yards	=	297.18 cm	=	2.97 m
3⅜ yards	=	308.61 cm	=	3.09 m
3½ yards	=	320.04 cm	=	3.20 m
3⅝ yards	=	331.47 cm	=	3.31 m
3¾ yards	=	342.90 cm	=	3.43 m
3⅞ yards	=	354.32 cm	=	3.54 m
4 yards	=	365.76 cm	=	3.66 m
4⅛ yards	=	377.19 cm	=	3.77 m
4¼ yards	=	388.62 cm	=	3.89 m
4⅜ yards	=	400.05 cm	=	4.00 m
4½ yards	=	411.48 cm	=	4.11 m
4⅝ yards	=	422.91 cm	=	4.23 m
4¾ yards	=	434.34 cm	=	4.34 m
4⅞ yards	=	445.76 cm	=	4.46 m
5 yards	=	457.20 cm	=	4.57 m

Annie's™ *Start With Scraps* is published by Annie's, 306 East Parr Road, Berne, IN 46711. Printed in USA. Copyright © 2009 DRG. All rights reserved. This publication may not be reproduced in part or in whole without written permission from the publisher.

RETAIL STORES: If you would like to carry this pattern book or any other Annie's publications, visit AnniesWSL.com

Every effort has been made to ensure that the instructions in this pattern book are complete and accurate. We cannot, however, take responsibility for human error, typographical mistakes or variations in individual work. Please visit AnniesCustomerCare.com to check for pattern updates.

ISBN: 978-1-59217-286-3